The Helpless Romantic

Falling in Love as an Aroace

poetry

ELLA KEYES

The Helpless Romantic

Front cover and back cover art by Ella Keyes
Author headshot by Christian Prime Guerra
Edited by Dr. Melanie Keyes

ISBN: 978-1-7383768-0-3
Printed in Canada

Published by Ella Keyes Books

For my Sunflower

You are my muse.
(Thank you for doing my laundry
while I worked on this book.)

Table of Contents

Introduction

The poems in this book were written over the course of seven years as I stumbled through the journey of finding love—and finding myself—as an aromantic asexual. For me, being aroace means I rarely experience romantic and sexual attraction. My feelings are complicated. I don't always understand them and it's taken a long time to realize that maybe I don't have to.

What matters to me is what I choose to do with my emotions, and where I want things to go. I feel most comfortable identifying as aromantic asexual—or aroace—however, my words and experiences probably don't fit neatly into any box, and neither do I. Through these poems, I'm just trying to express myself as best I can.

I've known I was asexual since I was 15 years old, but my identity didn't feel complete. It wasn't until third year university that I read a book with an aroace main character—Alice Oseman's *Loveless*—and everything clicked into place. This character brought my attention to the aromantic label and filled that missing piece in my identity.

Growing up, I didn't see any representation for asexual or aromantic people. Even now, these depictions are scarce. When I do see a character who is aromantic, asexual— or both—they almost always fall on the far end of the spectrum, where they are shown to experience a complete lack of attraction and no desire for a relationship. That representation is great, but I've also needed to see characters who I can relate to—characters who fall on other parts of spectrum.

Not all of the poems in this book are specifically about being aroace, but that part of me flows through all of my work. By no means do I represent the aromantic or asexual community, I'm just an aroace poet writing from my own experience. I am sure a lot of people who aren't aroace will relate to parts of this book, as I imagine some fellow aroaces won't relate at all. Still, I hope this book can help people like me feel heard. And for those who do find a piece of yourself in my writing in some way, I'm glad that I could share this with you.

The Helpless Romantic explores different types of love—romantic, platonic, aesthetic, familial, and my love of the world. In the past, I have discredited relationships I've had with people simply because they weren't romantic. Romantic love often takes such a centre stage, but I have since learned that whatever form love comes in, it is beautiful, real and worthy of consideration. All I can say is that these are my words, my thoughts, and my feelings.

These poems express my feelings and experiences with love and life. I'm a hopeless romantic who can't help but be infatuated with the idea of love. I have worshipped the written word for as long as I've been able to understand it. Captivated by the soft and passionate language, the dreaminess of love poetry caught my attention in high school and I was inspired to write my own. Love poems have always been an outlet for me as they help to hold the weight of my emotions and the heavy love I have for my partner, my friends, and the world around me.

When I found the person I wanted to be with, it took a lot of time to sort out where to go from there. Scared of these new feelings I had never experienced before, I struggled to figure out what kind of connection I wanted to have. For a long time, it didn't occur to me that I could create something that worked with someone who felt the way I do —someone who understood the type of love I needed and someone who wanted to build a life with me on our own terms.

Love is hard to define. All you can do is work with the people you care about to make sense of who you are to yourself and to each other. However we define ourselves or describe our experiences, we all simply start out as people and go from there. It's through fulfilling relationships—whether romantic, platonic, sexual or whatever we make them—that we find who we are. Only those bonds can bring us clarity and begin to make us feel like we belong.

I've kissed people before.
I always thought I wanted to open that door
but the movies show it wrong.
I've never had fireworks—
I've been told I might be cursed—
something disconnected in me.

It's supposed to make you feel—
the teeth clicks, gasps as mouths push and pull,
hands on necks,
arms,
waists,
sucking in tongues, cheeks, gums, skin,
lips bruised purple from passion.
I've seen the look in their eyes as we break apart—
giddy bliss—
I've felt their thundering hearts—
butterflies—
and I wonder why I felt nothing,
or worse, guilt.
I wonder why I can't find pleasure in this one thing
that everyone else seems to enjoy.
I wonder why I'm different,
heart sitting still in my chest
when it's meant to be glowing.
    - Disconnect

I like to pretend
I'm someone else.
It's how I've survived being myself.
From a distance, I watch a stranger.
Detachment can save a life.

I stare, empty, confused,
how could you hurt them so—
how could you let them go?

Never mind, it doesn't matter, it's not me.
     - Distance

I wanted to fall in love
like in the movies.
Love at first sight, destiny and
no doubts wondering if they're the one.
I could picture the slow motion petals
falling around me, and I wanted
that soft, warm spotlight.
I wanted to see my heart beat double speed
in a way that would make me sing in the shower
or dance half dressed around my room.
I wanted clean, perfect, easy,
and yet I couldn't picture what that meant or
what that would look like.
A fantasy on the outside
with no bones, no structure.
An empty relationship with an empty partner
and a lifeless me.
I could not put myself into those fairytales
without deconstructing myself,
peeling my guts out—the essence of
who I am, replaced with an idea—
the idea of love, mass-produced and
simply, not real.
I can still sing and dance,
have that love that I've desired,
but in my own style,
not flawed, but not perfection.
Real.
    - Fantasy Ideals

I love to look at the beauty of people.
True beauty is hard to explain,
but I see it in the way humans are made up of so many things,
like how a person's eyes sparkle when they laugh
or how their cheeks turn red with cold
or a nose scrunching in concentration.
I see it in small touches, hands reaching out to comfort
or to receive comfort,
polite smiles and nods in passing,
the way hair falls around a stranger's shoulder and frames their face.
I see it in clothing choice, self expression,
make-up done painstakingly.
The different kinds of walks, some full skip
others shuffle, shoes wearing into pavement.
I love the half sentences caught from phone calls in passing
leaving me full of curiosity, imagining a whole life out of
what it could mean, and
the unfettered dance moves that come like a possession
in night clubs, music so loud you can't hear yourself sing,
I love how people sing anyway.
I see such beauty in the kindness of others,
running to hold the door for a stranger,
helping to look for a missing earring in a café,
giving directions to the couple who most certainly look lost,
maps open on their phone but still in need of human assistance.
I watch the world around me look for hope, and I am looking too.
I find it in people.

    - The Beauty of People

She was made as though paint
had been thrown onto a canvas,
a messy kind of beauty you couldn't
look away from.
She drew constellations
on the edge of her notes,
connecting stars through bullet points
about medieval literature.
      - Classmate

Somehow the stars had a fault—
a mistake—
when they brought us together,
then pushed us away.
What was meant to be
dissolved into air.
And now all I can do
is pretend not to care
about you,
but I do.
And maybe I always will.
          - Nothing New

I gave you a piece of my heart to borrow.
Said keep it, until you get back.
But you never came back.

I used to keep track,
trading piece by piece of my heart
for ones belonging to others,
feeling pulled every which way
not fully complete without everyone I love.
But I can't always be with everyone I love,
and sometimes people don't come back.

I stand at the window when it rains
watching the drops drip patterns on the glass
and I think about the last time,
when we said goodbye
and I said, see you soon,
but there was no soon. And no next time.

I could let go and take my lost pieces back,
complete myself and stop thinking of you
so very often.
But feeling empty while you're gone
makes me feel more complete
than I would by giving up the love I have for you.
Your piece is yours to keep forever,
I have enough to spare.
        - Heart Pieces

Does it occur to you
that your smile
makes my heart swell?
Have you realized
that your voice soothes my soul?
Do you know
that your touch turns my cheeks red?
And when will you see
how much you mean to me?
     - Clueless

I've been broken,
and sewn back together
with messy, uneven stitches.
They say it's for the better.
But hold me in your arms,
'cause to tell you the truth,
I've never felt so put together
with anyone else.
        - Stitches

People unfold like books,
each page falling open in turn,
some fast, some slow.
But you,
you remain a mystery novel
written in riddles and invisible ink.
There is no hook there,
no blurb of explanation.
You let me read, paragraphs, one at a time,
slowly, letting me know you better and
better with every new line.
      - Mystery Man

I still can't tell you,
I'm just too afraid.
Afraid of what? That
things will change?
Because
I like your smile,
I like your beautiful laugh,
I like the way your arms feel around me.
Our relationship is so carefree.
So what if I'm wrong?
What if you don't feel the same?
I don't want to scare you away.
    - I Don't Like Being So Unsure

Tell me if I'm going crazy—
if I'm seeing things.
In the past I have built up a shield of doubt
to save me from misery.
Now,
I'm starting to sense we want
the same things,
that maybe you can also see
a future with me.

I crave the space between your arms,
waking up to your smile,
falling asleep to your voice.
I've never had this much hope,
never felt this close to
the type of relationship I've craved.
I've started to fall—
teetering on the edge—
and I need to know
if you'll be there to jump with me.

   - Let Me Know If You're In

The way you look at me with so much love,
oh! How it hurts my heart.
Would I prefer that you close yourself off from me
and never say another kind word?
Is it better to never talk to you again,
knowing we may part ways?
Or should I spend every moment I can with you,
until then,
despite the impending heartbreak?
    - My Dilemma

There is such a risk in loving.
You thread together your most vulnerable parts,
stringing them with the finest silk,
but the problem with finer things
is how easily they break.
And they must break,
whether you are accepted, or rejected
the string will snap and you will stumble back,
for all to see the full picture.

They must see you, these other beings to
whom you give yourself,
and that is a great fear.
To be loved is to be known
although we wish to hide,
staying hidden for all eternity.
A paradox of keeping ourselves to ourselves,
yet wanting to have someone to share the load.

There will always be people who
makes you believe they deserve
to see the things that others cannot.
You will debate pros and cons,
and upon revealing yourself to them
you will find out if it was worth it,
or not.

The secret you may have forgotten
is that it always is,
whether it hurts more than fire

or makes your heart sing,

you can say that you tried,

and you can say that you learned.

Proudly I will give my heart,

I will risk it all,

for at the end of it all,

at least I can say I was brave.

    - Showing

My body does not feel like my own.
There is just this strange disconnect,
my skin is cold and foreign to me.
I can't feel it when I trace my veins.
My feet take numb steps
and I stumble.
I am someone else
inside my brain,
so let me belong to you,
he who takes me in
and helps me feel
whole.
       - Belonging

Are you afraid to touch me?
You tell me how much you want to,
and then pull away at the chance.
A mumbled apology for
a brush against my chest,
a sharp sigh for
an accidental graze of inner thigh.
Wide eyes darting to mine,
fearful that you'll scare me away.
But you never will.
        - I'm Yours If You Want Me

I crave your hands on my skin.
I've let my walls down, and let you in.
Gentle arms caressing,
your fingertips trace the lines that hurt most.
Lying softly on your chest, so peacefully,
I feel like I've found my home.
Your kisses find the parts I'd rather leave alone.
Every little compliment helps me love myself again,
of course I let you in.

    - In

All I have is sun.
Just you, and the sun.
Smiling in the sun,
waving to me.
How glad I am that the sun was shining that day
so that I have it now frozen in my memory,
here in my heart where no one can take it away.
Sparkling sun.
You were so beautiful in the sunshine.

    - Sunshine

And I say words aren't my thing.
Though they cover the pages and pages
and pages of
every notebook that I own,
flowing through computer files,
covering the walls of my home,
braided into my veins,
buried deep beneath my skin,
the same words I drink in.

But now I'm standing here before you
and I can't find a single thing to say.
Except that I've never felt
this type of way.
So let me show you instead.
> \- Words on a Page are Easier Than Words Said

Touch me again
with your gentle fingertips,
your measured gaze
keeping me locked in sight,
eyes filled with worry
that I will back away,
but I'm not going anywhere.
     - Feel Me

I want to take you to my favourite places.
The pho restaurant at the end of my street,
the lake at the other side of the park,
the market where I buy pretty rocks,
the farm with baby goats in the spring
where you can buy fresh goat cheese.
So that there is nowhere in my life
that you haven't been.
  - Know Me

Just us
in nature.
Under swaying trees.
We watch
the birds play.
And busy buzzing bees.
The sunlight in your eyes
dances when you smile.
I wish we could stay here,
but we only have a little while.
    - Just Us in Nature

I cannot get over your beauty.
Those big, brown, almond eyes that look up
at me expectantly as your head rests on my chest.
The way the coils of your hair fall across the nape of your neck
or how when I lift those same coils to the side
I can see the ones beneath, slightly looser but just as pretty.
The hair on your chest, your back, your abdomen that is soft against my
skin,
ears that remain half hidden, oval and elegant in shape.
A soft nose and full lips I wish to press my own face against,
round cheeks that shift into that perfect smile,
concealed slightly by a well-kept and handsome beard.
Long fingers that wrap around mine, fitting there like puzzle pieces.
The dark mole on the right side of your ribs,
the small birthmark just under your collar,
the scar on your cheek—I remember when you had stitches.
The roughness of your hands,
the beauty mark under your eye.
        - Your Beauty

He smells like vanilla in the subtlest of ways.
Vanilla mixed with tree bark in a morning after rain.
And then again he doesn't smell like those things at all,
but more their memories
as if someone took a picture of the rainy scene and
the photography breathed life into it.
Perhaps it's vanilla cookies, the doughy sweetness,
the freshness like sun rising, and dew.
I am trying so hard to place it,
my nose buried deep in the thick fabric of his hoodie.
Recognition comes and goes,
one second I am certain of vanilla
the next, not so sure.
There is carrot oil in his beard
and coconut shampoo in his hair,
the hint of soft deodorant, extra fresh.
And spices linger on his clothes
from meals cooked at home.
His hands smell like my goat milk soap,
but beneath this all, something more,
something a bit like vanilla.
     - Scent of Vanilla

It's strange how we pretend to know each other,
these strangers I meet in elevators,
picking up conversations that were never left off.

I love listening to languages I don't understand.
Like music, emotions flow
and though I cannot tell what is being said,
I feel it fully.
       - Snippets in Passing

We are both wearing corduroys
sitting opposite on the bus.
A bag of Miss Vickie's
sticks out of your groceries.
You do not know
that I have one in my backpack too.
- Parallels

I would know you for a day.
I would know you for an hour,
for a minute.
I would see you only once—
a glance in passing—
there only in my most precious daydreams.
I would know you from across a crowded room
never to reach you.
All that is better than
never knowing you
not once
not at all.
        - Worth It

My hands in yours,
dim TV light,
I look over into your deep eyes.
A little smile creeps from the side
of your mouth,
I'm looking for the words
but I don't need them now,
This is the part where we're supposed to kiss.
But we don't.

Your lips look nice, I won't lie.
Outside beauty to match the inside.
I like the way you feel against my skin,
I could stare at you all day just taking you in.
I want to be as close to you as I can
but oh man,
the thought of your lips on mine
twists up my insides—
not like butterflies,
not like I'm being shy,
like something caught in the
back of my throat.
I'm scared and I don't know why.

I just don't understand the appeal,
mouths on mouths like a vacuum seal,
it doesn't stir anything within me,
or feel magical, fantastical—
like fireworks, they say—
filled with passion,

yearning, yet
nothing. Nothing for me.
I don't see what they see.

I like your lips on my skin,
tender kisses on my cheek,
goodnight kisses on my forehead,
I like your mouth taking me in.
A sign of lovingness, of care.
I don't know what it would
feel like to kiss you. I
wonder. Are you
wondering too?
          - Stirrings

I trace the lines of your back
in careful motions, pouring my love out through my fingers,
hoping my touch will convey just how much I care.
I press your body to me
feeling the warmth flow through your chest and into mine,
the pressure of you holds me down like a weighted blanket—
light and comfortable, and safe.
Secure.
You ask why I hold you so close
and I cannot answer.
There are too many words I could use to describe the
madness in my heart when I look into your sweet eyes,
or the beautiful longing I feel to reach out and touch your skin,
or the ache inside my chest to always have you near,
growing unbearable when you are away
until finally you are back
and my arms can take you up again.

But I know there is always a goodbye.
So I hold you while I can, and I hold you close.
Close enough to feel your heart beat, feel your breath on my cheek,
and know that I was lucky enough to find a spot in your arms.
        - Weighted Blanket

I want to live in a home that's filled with light.
Let the walls be painted bright yellow or white,
I want open windows and a summer breeze
blowing back delicate curtains as I gaze
out at our trees.
I want bookcases everywhere
filled to bursting with books,
piles more beside my bed, my cozy armchair,
piles and piles all throughout.
I want deep couches and soft blankets,
and my own reading nook, plush pillows.
I want sun streaks and candle light,
warm, warm all around me.
      - Dream of a Home

My love is beautiful like the ocean.
Soft in his smile the way the
clouds break over quiet waves,
deep in his heart like the plunging, bottomless blue.
Strong as the waves that crash into each other and then relent,
and as gentle as the tides that kiss the shore.
He has soft, mysterious eyes that call to mind
breathtaking cliffs on a cloudy day,
their deep browns dancing in the half light of the hiding sun.
The curves of his brows are stern,
hard in concentration when he works
but never lacking kindness,
like the rocky beaches my bare feet tread delicately upon.
When he laughs it is like sunlight on water,
the warm glow of his skin mirrored in the dancing light,
the sound is that of rain on a calm day,
smooth, loud laughter,
music that echoes the sound of the sea in my ears.
    - My Love is Like the Ocean

Our bodies
together, up close glimpses
chest to chest
thigh to hip,
your hands on my waist.
The frantic rise and
fall
of our bellies.
Two into one.
        - Balancing

We're there,
somewhere in time,
trapped in a perfect moment.
I still sit in your arms,
your head in the crook of my neck.
One beautiful piece out of time
where we laugh and we smile,
staying forever, just like that,
through a rose coloured filter.
I can see your hands on my skin, I'm breathing you in,
you kiss me so lightly, I'm holding you tightly,
the heat of our bodies so warm and inviting.
I shut my eyes hoping to savour every detail
but it's okay,
because we will always be that way,
hand in hand, comfortable and close,
perfectly cool, breathing in deeply,
your fingertips running lazy up and down my arms,
I squeeze your waist, gazing up at your face
forever in that moment frozen in time.

    - Somewhere Frozen in Time

I like the way he grabs me.
Gentle with his touch.
I like how he asks me
for my everything
without asking too much.
- You Shall Receive

We couldn't have been more opposite,
and yet so the same.
Our souls recognized each other
before I knew your name.
Somehow we've stuck together
through the challenges we've faced.
The string connecting our hearts
will never fray.
        - I Know Your Soul

Rough hands searching
to find my softest parts,
the utmost delicacy for hands so strong.
I am cradled in your tender arms,
held as though I am a flower,
just enough pressure to feel safe,
secure, with room to grow.
At home inside your walls.

     - Sown

His soft words are
different from anything I've known.
His gentle hands
would never let me come to harm.
From his lips
sweet, caring words
telling me how beautiful
I am,
inside and out.

This body,
which feels not like my own,
deserves my love
but time and again
I cannot seem to give it.
But I am not alone,
I am loved.
And I am learning
to love myself
just a little bit.

I used to think
that I wasn't good.
That my heart was cold
from casting all away in
hopes of protecting myself.
But I am worthy of love.

    - This is No Simple Thing

Slipping wet feet into
socks after a day at the beach
feels exciting
like breaking a small rule
or sitting cross-legged on a grassy field
wrapped in blankets
watching fireworks.
It feels like the essence
of summer.

      - Summertime

I did not want the wasp to die,
so I came up with an excuse.
What if when you go to snuff it out,
it stings you?
She let the insect go with a fervent agreeing nod.

I watched the wasp fly away
guilty of the fear I had reinforced on its behalf.
    - The Wasp

Do you need me?
Whispered gently in your ear,
soft—
barely audible—
fear faded words that
found the cracks in my heart
and pulled at its cords.

Your arms held my waist.
Delicate
gentle
grasping,
as if I could float away.
I felt your breath on my neck,
the ghost of a kiss.

Warm bodies
made to fit together in
peaceful embrace,
shooting stars falling into place
as hands found the smalls of backs,
and passionately, you whispered back,
Of course I do.
     - Love Poem

My love for you is devoted hands
against your face,
the way I rest my chin between your
collarbone and the slope of your shoulder,
how I hold you back when it's
time for you to go.

Your love for me is tiny kisses
on my thighs,
the way you hold me tight
but soft,
how you take my hands in yours
when I'm nervous,
transferring to me the strength that I need.
    - The Ways We Love

There will always be our names
etched into the old bridge downtown—
I suppose unless they tear it down,
or the frayed bracelets we wore all summer
and now keep in boxes
the ones that weren't lost,
torn off in sleep, or unravelled and forgotten
on the soccer field.
There will always be the polaroids
that never quite turned out
and the letters, and the sand in my beach bag
that I will never be able to fully remove.

    - Signs That We Were Here

The early morning air was too cold,
far too cold as the warmth of sleep
seeped out of my skin and into the darkness.
The deep blue of the predawn sky lit our way
in dim light, the hard concrete underfoot
a firm reminder of this uncomfortable goodbye.
My hand grasped yours and all I could think about
was the safe, warm bed
we had left minutes before.
I fought everything in me that screamed to turn around,
and when we arrived at the station, no bus in sight,
I felt hope rise in my chest. Minute after
minute ticked by, no bus in sight,
as our breath puffed cool in the air
and my cheek crushed against your chest.
Ten minutes I stood there,
holding your hand and hoping
the bus wouldn't come.
    - Leaving

Let me write poems about the things that scare me
so that when I am old, I can look back
and think how silly it was
to dread the future.
How trivial it will seem to fear a setting sun
or the way my face will change,
I will laugh at how I grasped at youth while I still had it,
now unbothered by my lack of it.

I do not wish to grow into someone who dreads
the turning of my age, unwilling to add a number
to my birthday cake.
I would prefer not to give time so much power
as to consider myself depleted after thirty,
a creased and deflated balloon according to
cosmetic propaganda and the sour old men who sell it.
I would rather throw my little fears onto a page
and let them sit, collecting dust, waiting
for me to find them again when I'm old.
	- Time Moves Still

My bed feels colder now,
the covers feel too thin.
Nothing can compare to
your arms on my skin.
Nothing is as soft,
or as comforting,
just let me drift off
and dream of you
holding me.
Let me sleep peacefully
shrouded in the safety that you bring,
feeling your warmth against my cheek,
letting your chest rise and
fall opposite mine.
Apart from you all I do is dream.
- Pretending

A secret from your lips
touches my ear,
I whisper back that I'm right here
but you fade away into the night,
just a figment of my thoughts,
soon as arriving, taking flight.

      - I Dream That You're With Me

Life is made up
of missing people.
There will always be a
part of my heart
in some other place.
I wish the good times
were enough
to take the pain of
parting away.
Sometimes it seems to be
the wrong choice
to let people get close to me,
and although I know
the ways of the world—
how nothing is meant to last—
it's often difficult to stay in
the moment
without thinking that this will
one day be the past.

       - It Gets Harder Every Time

The bakery by the park where I'd buy blueberry pie.
The candy shop across from my elementary school
that I would run to at lunch.
The old playground that burned down
where I used to spend hours after school.
The school library
where I discovered my love of books.
The chip truck that sold jalapeño poutine.
The diner at the end of the street of my first home.
The Mexican restaurant that had amazing churros.
The cozy bookstore that moved a few blocks away.
The shop that sold steamed pork buns that I would eat
when I was little.
The mall that only exists in my deepest memories—
I can't remember its name or where it was.
The ice cream stand where I would lift my little brother up
to the counter so he could see.
The hot dog shop that sold mini, sweet tasting hot dogs and
give stickers to the kids.
The art studio where I had lessons,
where we would sit on the rug during break for story time
and eat saltine crackers.

    - Places That Don't Exist Anymore

I watch movies
ones I've seen a thousand times before,
where I swear I can recite the lines word for word
but on every try I get at least one wrong.
I can lose myself in a book for weeks,
reading twelve words at a time,
barely stopping to eat or sleep,
enthralled by every line.
Sometimes stories make me feel like
I could do something with my life.
Then I get into phases where I can't even look at a page,
months go by without a chapter read,
and I kick myself, guilty for all the time wasted
and the characters unmet.
I find times when I have no interest in watching anything,
choosing to mindlessly scroll on my phone instead
and I wonder if I'm wasting my life.
But the calm voice in the back of my mind tells me that
life isn't measured in numbers of books
or stories consumed,
and sometimes you need breaks,
and to follow your heart,
or follow your brain,
follow the part of you that lets you rest,
without guilt.
You'll get back out there soon.
    - Brain Slumps

There is room
enough
beside me.
Just enough
for you
to fill.
Wrap me up
in strong arms
feel my skin
with kind hands
waves washing worries away
as my head rests
on your chest,
the tides will slow
for only a moment
and all that will matter is us.
  - Don't You See You Have My Heart?

Your thumbprint on my neck
stains purple against my skin,
I love the quiet way you gasp
as your arms brace us both
and our glistening skin
catches in the soft light.
I find a lock of your
curls in my bed
the next morning,
and between that and the
fading thumbprint you left,
I feel you close to me still.
    - Remnants

The leaves on the trees are
turning orange,
red, brown.
Soon they will start to fall to the ground.
It makes me consider how far I've come,
and all the things I've grown from.
I see asters peeking out from the leafy floor,
shortly to be buried once more,
and squirrels scurrying to scavenge for the last acorns.
I love how the wind turns cold and harsh, how
the sky can't seem to choose between clear
and brooding.
Flowers wilt, drooping petals that fall
one
by one.
Branches shed their foliage, become bare
as birds spread their wings and fly away.
There's such a strange beauty in this dying and decay.
    - To Fall

Let me take a walk with you
under trees, autumn leaves.
Eyes turned up towards skies of blue
filled with clouds, floating down.
Let me take this walk with you,
through the paths that we've wandered past
for many years.

We'll find a field of sunflowers,
and they'll remind me of you.
Break one by the stem,
put in it my hand,
I'll tuck it in my belt.
I'll take it home, put it in a vase
filled with water and let it stay there
until it wilts, the petals dropping off.

Let me take a walk with you
under trees, autumn leaves,
forever under that sky of blue.
     - Autumn Walk

I don't know what others feel.
Or what I'm supposed to feel,
I just know that I haven't felt it
the way I've heard it described.
I can call these feelings love and desire
and have that be true—
but they may not be the same experience.
What I want and what I feel I need, do not line up,
I often wonder about this magnetic pull described by others
and I wonder if I'm doing this wrong.
Does it really matter
the wanting of my mind versus
the wanting of my body?
Who cares where these feelings come from—if anywhere at all.
I know who I want and how,
I know our goals align, that we are happy.
I've tried too long to put it into words,
This lack of feelings,
This abundance of wants.
I struggle to explain it all.
I don't want to explain it at all.
I see the irony
in being an aromantic love poet.
But I've grown up on fairytales
and I'm hopelessly—and helplessly—
infatuated with the world of love.
    - Aroace Love Poet

Curving lines of ink
spinning intricate designs,
I will wrap myself in gold
letting fabric spill from
my delicate shoulders,
over every inch of skin
until I become art myself,
draped in all the finery I deserve,
from the dark black lines I have had
drawn onto me, to the bright colours
that I paint over my face,
the jewels I will hang from my neck
and wrists, and all the silk, cashmere,
and satin my heart desires.
 - I Will Cover Myself in Art

There's a street lamp
shining through my window
casting restless shadows on the walls,
dark leaves blowing softly
around my room.

My eyes are wide open,
my head is full of thoughts.
I tried to get some sleep tonight,
but all hope of that is lost.
The night is quiet,
there's a slight chill in the air.
Time must be ticking away
but right now, I don't care.
The thoughts in my head
are all thoughts of you.

A streetcar goes by outside,
there's a rumble on the tracks.
Light fades in and
out of view, from
passing cars.

If I never know another night
to slip off into dreams
without a fight,
I will be grateful for nights
like these,
peaceful, and

full of thoughts of you.
>   - Thinking of You Again

He wanted everything.
The sun, the moon
the stars.
He wanted storms,
quiet meadows
and cool rain.
He wanted emotions
in every form.
I was a piece of the sky and
the earth
torn apart and told I burned too bright,
sang too loud, talked too much.
But he rejoiced when he found me—
calling out perfection,
he said I am enough.
That I am more than enough.
    - Let Me Be Your Everything

Let me give you my heart
in a piece of cake shared
in the small, crowded booth near the window,
in a sunny afternoon down by the lake
where the brightness of the water blinds us
but not as brilliantly as your smile,
in the texts that I send saying *thinking of you,*
with tears that roll off my chin as I count down
the days left until I see you again, staring at your
face on the distant screen of my laptop,
my heart telling me to reach out and grab you,
my brain knowing you aren't physically here.
Let me give you my heart in nights spent stealing covers,
in sleepy mornings where I slide out of bed
careful not to nudge you awake.
Let me give you the pieces of my love in
these small ways in which I can.
    - For You

I hated kissing until there was you.
I couldn't wrap my head around
that kind of affection with anyone else.
I tried to, but I felt nothing.
No pull to the other person's body,
no spark where our lips met, or from
wandering hands.
There wasn't even disgust, or aversion,
just complete apathy and
emptiness.
A pit inside me wondering why
nothing ever clicked.

Then there was you, the first time
my heart opened to another,
the first time I was able to feel
something.
With you it means *something*,
it doesn't need to make me feel any
certain feelings, no pressure to
understand it,
just us, together,
doing what feels right.
      - Until You

There are a million things I want to say to you.
A thousands words throughout the day,
but you have stuff to do.
I think of the smallest thoughts that
I want you to hear,
I think of conversations we've had and
parts I want to make clear,
parts I want to laugh at again, things I forgot to say.
I'm just thinking of you.
All the time.
　　　- On My Mind

I fell in love.
Not in an infatuated storm,
but slow.
Gradual, and strong,
building up this quiet hope from deep roots
I have taken time to sow.
We have been a long time coming
with every touch small
and delicately placed,
with darting glances and feigned awkwardness
as we pretended not to want so much
while wanting so very much.

      - Fresh Love

I thought I was exaggerating you in my mind,
adding filtered lenses to memories, but
here I am after I've come to find that
you are even better than everything I imagined.
Traipsing through the thick underbrush of our friendship,
I dared to push borders and traverse deadly ravines,
slaying my fears and anxieties of getting too close,
to come to a place where I truly know you
and here I found my oasis.
    - Discovery

He left bruises on my thighs in the most perfect way,
purple ovals matching his fingertips,
he kissed my belly,
my breasts,
my wrists—
butterflies from his lips,
hair brushing against my skin.
Lighting up this body I'm in.
      - Butterflies

I want strawberry kisses on my thighs and
I want to write you poems.
I want to make plans and
keep them, keep you pressed
into the soft parts of me,
tucked away and mine.
Forever mine.
    - Wishes

I've measured my time in you
from moment to moment.
I've counted the years,
relying on when I can see you again
to keep track of the days,
I've measured long nights in your carefree words
and early mornings in your laughter.
I've counted the weeks that we were apart
and marked my calendar with your return,
hours passing that kept me watching for your call.
And when we are together again, all time
stops.

    - Timepiece

I'm the poet.
I've written many love poems of different kinds
to friends, family—him.
Never thinking I'd receive one myself.
He wrote me a poem,
inspired by my work—
the words I sing to him
about my love.
A poem for me
full of the love of my form,
my being as is held in his eyes
and the way I move to him,
as if I am the whole world,
as if he is the world and I am the sun.
He talks of me like a dazzling jewel
which he holds in his hands,
and with such beautiful words I know
two things:
how much he cares, and
that I may now have new competition.
 - I Am the Sun to Your Moon

Today I stood in front of the mirror
and noticed for the first time
the pretty shine in my eyes,
the way my hair loops back behind uneven ears,
the slight half smile befitting one
who has looked at their own face too often
and yet not often enough.

I skip when I walk.
There's a small bounce in my step
that I never noticed until I was told
that it makes me feel refreshing—
carefree—to others.
Really I'm nervous, anxious,
with too much energy.

My hands always find themselves
in front of my face
when my emotions are too strong.
The instinct is to cover up,
fingers curled in fists, chin tilted down.
My feelings always feel like too much.
I know it shows in my features that
I don't seem to know exactly
how to let them out.

I am trying to write myself love poems.
I like to add a rose coloured lens to
the people in my life, or perhaps
more of a sepia one—perfect for jagged memories.

So here I have painted myself in a small way
with my flaws, with
an untidy style to match my chaos.
Trying, trying, trying.
	- Self Love Poem

My body is not a temple.
It is a home,
not meant to be vigilantly monitored
and kept in pristine condition
but to be lived in.
I'd rather a soft worn couch
than cool marble benches,
I will not let my body sit idle
stuck in false perfection
afraid to look anything other than holy.
There will be cobwebs unswept,
chipped colourful cups,
books with bent spines,
plants half dead in the windows,
ragged blankets that still hold warmth,
the corners will be less than clean
and the floors, still dirty from last week's rain.
I think you will find that divinity
is more likely to be found in the heart
than in an empty room,
so like the goddesses before me
I will live life unafraid of the consequences of time
and drink my fill.
     - Home

I wanted to be someone who could give themself
effortlessly. Love and give love, creating as openly as
the muses who perform and delight.
I wished to give more of myself than I truly wanted
and having tried that route, discovered
that my heart does not follow that path.
There is more than one way to win a war,
multiple roads to victory, and the peace I long for
will come to me on my own terms.

    - Of Athena

Your hairs are in my bed and
I'm in love with you.
Not just my bed,
I find them on my clothes,
the bottom of my socks,
the carpet in my living room,
in my own hair.
I love you when you're half asleep,
the way your long eyelashes flutter,
your arm draped across your forehead.
I want to keep waking up with you,
the warmth of sleep clinging to our pyjamas
as we eat breakfast and I make my coffee.

The scent of your room reminds me of autumn,
and I like it more than my own because of the
way the light comes in through the window
next to your bed.
It's so bright here, bright enough to dream.
I think of the future and what colours to paint our walls.
We will have a yellow kitchen
and windows that let all the light in.
I'm not one to care for plants but I can see me trying,
partially wilted greenery along the walls.
We will collect objects that make us happy,
weird trinkets and slightly salacious art.

We will have flowers for every occasion
kept in elegant vases on the kitchen counter
so that each morning I can be greeted by soft petals.

I will fill our home with sunflowers,
bright oranges and yellows,
so that they draw in the sun
and we'll live in such a brightness,
and I will continue to find your hairs everywhere
everyday.
      - Sunflower

Acknowledgments

I have so much gratitude towards everyone who supported me in the process of writing this book. It has truly been a wonderful journey. Sixteen-year-old Ella would be shocked that their quickly jotted poems about feelings for a classmate and friend have ended up in a book. Maybe they'd be a little embarrassed too.

I loved collecting and editing my poems from years ago, it brought so many feelings back to me, and the new poems I wrote for this book felt like responses to the old. I'm proud of how far I've come in discarding the uncertainty and fear that used to surround my thoughts on identity. This has been a huge learning experience in so many ways.

To start, I want to thank my lovely partner, Christian, who was the inspiration for this book. Thank you for always encouraging my passion—you push me to write and keep writing. You've supported me by studying next to me, making me food, and putting up with my usual shenanigans. I will always appreciate the attention with which you listen to my poetry, and the smiles and laughs I get in response. Thank you for the hours you spent helping me research the publishing process, reading and explaining legal stuff to me, troubleshooting how to design a cover, and helping me bounce around ideas. Thank you so much for taking my headshot, I had a fun time posing for a million pictures and I love how they turned out.

Thank you to my mom, Dr. Melanie Keyes (Dr. Mom), who is my number one editor and biggest fan. Thank you for reading this book over and over again, and editing the many different drafts. From catching my mistakes to helping me rework my introduction countless times, you've done so much for me. I appreciate all the feedback that you don't hold out on or sugarcoat. (Even though your notes always apologize for being too harsh, I promise you never are!) I love how eagerly you awaited my first draft and how you called me after reading it to tell me how much you like my book. Thank you for always inspiring me to take risks, work hard, and follow my dreams.

Thank you to Rachel, who sent me edits and comments. I really appreciate the time you took to look over my work. Thank you to Freja, Tiff and Julia, who sent me their thoughts on my first draft. Thank you to Sandy Robson who met with me and shared his publishing experiences. Thank you to my dad, Denis Keyes, for giving me printing advice, explaining the publishing process, and answering my one hundred questions.

I'd like to thank everyone who supported me. All my friends and family who got excited when I told them I was publishing, and of course my wonderful readers who have made my dreams possible by choosing my book.

Dear Reader,

Thank you for purchasing my first book! I am grateful for the support of every one of my readers. If you have time to leave a review on Goodreads or Amazon, I would greatly appreciate it. You can also check out my Instagram @ella.keyes.writer

Ella Keyes is a Canadian, nonbinary poet and writer who was born and raised in Toronto. In 2023, they received a bachelor's degree in English and creative writing from the University of Guelph, where they spent two years as an editor and writer for the Guelph chapter of Her Campus. Besides throwing their thoughts on paper, Ella enjoys reading, photography, hiking and singing. *The Helpless Romantic* is their first book.

www.ingramcontent.com/pod-product-compliance
Lightning Source LLC
Chambersburg PA
CBHW051815050726
47598CB00006B/2568